Suicide

Understanding
and Intervening

Resources for Changing Lives

A Ministry of
THE CHRISTIAN COUNSELING AND
EDUCATIONAL FOUNDATION
Glenside, Pennsylvania

RCL Ministry Booklets
Susan Lutz, Series Editor

Suicide

Understanding and Intervening

Jeffrey S. Black

P&R
PUBLISHING
P.O. BOX 817 • PHILLIPSBURG • NEW JERSEY 08865-0817

Printed in the United States of America

Library of Congress Cataloging-in-Publication Data

Black, Jeffrey S., 1954-
    Suicide : understanding and intervening / Jeffrey S. Black.
        p.   cm. — (Resources for changing lives)
    Includes bibliographical references.
    ISBN 10: 0-87552-693-4
    ISBN 13: 978-0-87552-693-5
    1. Suicide. 2. Suicide—Religious aspects—Christianity. 3. Suicide—Prevention. I. Title. II. Series.

HV6545.B53 2003
362.28—dc21   2003043359

It was a dreary February afternoon when an old friend called me. He wanted to talk about suicide. His wife had recently tidied up the house, swallowed everything in the medicine cabinet, and slashed her wrists and forearms. He was hoping I could explain it all to him, to clear up his confusion and nullify some of his pain. I wanted to say something powerful and profound, but the fact was I had nothing profound to declare.

As a pastor, I can't think of many things I like less than conducting the funeral of a believer who has committed suicide. The paradoxes pile up on top of each other. Do I talk about the providence and sovereignty of God the way I would when talking about the death of a child? That hardly makes sense. Do I talk about the power and presence of God in the midst of suffering? Yes, if I am talking to those attending the funeral. But what about the victim? Was there insufficient grace for this believer? That hardly seems likely. Even the term "suicide victim" is paradoxical. Certainly, the paradox is felt as friends and family eulogize this believer's love for family and service to Christ. In our hearts, someone must go on trial, but who? The person who cut his life short? We who somehow failed him? Perhaps God or his Word?

The suicide of a Christian is no more tragic than the suicide of an unbeliever, but it *is* more puzzling. After all, believers are promised new life in Christ and a living hope, while non-Christians do not know Christ and are not indwelt by the Holy Spirit. Yet the worldviews of the suicidally depressed Christian and non-Christian are remarkably similar. The experience of unbearable pain, interpersonal alienation, and hopelessness is similar. The struggle with unmet felt needs and the belief that there are no solutions to their problems is the same. The difference seems to be that non-Christians have no light or truth, and so seek help in what we view as idols, while Christians have light and truth but don't keep their eyes on these things. The paradox is brought into full focus when a suicidal Christian wants to know if she will lose her salvation if she kills herself. The contradiction in her thinking—that the same God who has the power to condemn her eternally doesn't have the power to help her now—seems lost on her.

The thoughts and emotional experiences that lead some to suicide flow from the same spring as the mildest depression. The same biblical truths that explain mild sadness also explain suicide. Having said that, the intention to commit suicide is a crisis that requires us to be familiar with the various indicators that someone plans to take his life. We also need to know how to intervene when someone appears suicidal. I hope to offer some guidelines in this booklet.

The Inner World of the Suicidal Person

Let's begin by describing the thought life and emotions of a suicidal person. But remember that these descriptions are not explanations. Psychological pain, interpersonal alienation, and hopelessness are not the ultimate reasons why someone commits suicide. Though the pain of depression can be suffocating, our wills and our moral values are part of every aspect of our lives. Even when there is a biological component to the depression, our interpretations of our experiences—and our responses to them—are rooted in the thoughts and desires of our hearts. According to the Bible, what finally determines our experiences and choices is whether we see our lives through the lens of our relationship with Jesus Christ. In that light, we can see that suicide is the act of a sinful heart; it cannot be reduced to psychological experiences.

This can be difficult to remember because of suicide's tragic dimensions. When someone takes his life, we look for ways to explain the choice. It is a mystery to be solved, and the chief witness cannot testify, often leaving few clues. Therefore, we often regard the description as the explanation: "He killed himself because he was hopeless." "She killed herself because she couldn't forgive herself." Too often, however, we fail to penetrate the veil of hopelessness to see a heart that had drifted from the place of truth and peace. In that regard, Berkouwer's observation about sin's fundamental senselessness is appropriate.

> Therefore, since every "unriddling" of sin implies a discovery of "sense" where no sense can possibly be found, the very notion of an "unriddling" is impossible. One cannot find sense in the senseless and meaning in the meaningless.
>
> All of this does not imply that sin is any less a power or an influence on re-

ality, or any less "real." What it does imply is that sin cannot be explained in terms of its component factors and cannot be made "explicable." We have seen that every initiative in that direction can only end up, unavoidably, in self-excuse. . . . The senselessness of man's sin is the riddle of man's sin. . . . Sin is enigmatic and inexplicable simply because it has no presuppositions and no cause and no real motive at all.[1]

Descriptions of the suicidal state of mind do not finally explain the act. We must consider people in relation to God.

Created and Covenantal Beings

Man is a created and covenantal being. In 2 Corinthians 4, Paul describes believers as "jars of clay," as common, unspectacular pottery made useful and valuable by the riches of Christ "contained" inside. We are made common to ensure that God receives the honor for what is done (4:7; cf. Judg. 7:2–3), but we are also subject to hardship. Most of us have cried out in the midst of a dark night of the soul. Paul, too, describes moments of anguish

(4:7–9). In the end, however, he calls them "light and momentary afflictions" (4:17). Why?

First, because his whole life, even his greatest difficulties, is lived *purposely* (4:10–12, 15). He willingly endures hardship because of the fruit born out of his suffering. Second, his whole life is lived in relation to *the future* (4:17–18). Affliction "becomes" light (bearable) and momentary (endurable) when actively contrasted with what is being stored up: "Our light and momentary troubles are achieving for us an eternal glory that far outweighs them all" (4:17). Third, Paul lives his whole life by the daily renewing of *the Holy Spirit* (4:16; cf. Eph. 3:16; Col. 1:11). In other texts, Paul describes the renewing as strengthening and empowering. Notice that the renewing is a renewing *to* something. He is strengthened daily to attack the tasks God has set before him. Renewing is not a good feeling, but a capacity to endure what comes as a result of suffering for Christ.

Paul makes a similar observation in Philippians 3:10: "I want to know Christ and the power of his resurrection and the fellowship of sharing in his sufferings, becoming like him in his death." That is especially illuminating since suicidal thought typically arises from the cumulative disappointments of life. In adopting the mindset of Christ, the weight of the most difficult trial does not crush Paul; confusion does not lead to despair; and persecution is not experienced as abandonment (4:8–9). This is what it means to be a covenantal being.

Suicide *is* a sinful act. Because it is born out of pain or sorrow, I find it difficult at times to discuss this sinful aspect with family and friends. Most of the time it is obvious and doesn't need emphasis. However, I am more than willing to discuss suicide's sinful dimension with a depressed individual, but not primarily to talk him out of it. Pointing out that suicide is sinful has limited value as a deterrent. However, as a way to explore the person's worldview, talking about suicide as sin is pure gold. The fact that a suicidal person often sees himself as a powerless victim, while the Bible calls suicide sin, reveals the shift that must occur in his thinking. My goal is not simply to get the person to repent over a specific act of lawbreaking (suicide), but to undermine his pattern of sinfully self-centered rationalization. Suicide is a profoundly tragic act, but it is ultimately an expression of self-centeredness contrary to our position as creatures responsible to a Creator.

This self-centeredness shows itself when

"life is unbearable and I need to escape" becomes the dominating thought. As someone moves towards the decision to end his life, he must also explain away the consequences of his action. He must minimize concerns about family members who are left to deal with the personal loss, added responsibility, guilt, and regrets. So the person diminishes the effects of the loss: "They don't need me now; they won't miss me when I'm gone." He overestimates the survivors' ability to deal with the loss: "The children are strong; they'll get over it." He nullifies their right to experience loss: "They will understand that my pain was unbearable. They would do the same if they were me." In these ways, the person will rationalize his decision to kill himself.

In addition, consider this: Not everyone who is depressed is suicidal, and not everyone who is suicidal is depressed. Bitterness, anger, and an unwillingness to forgive are common features of suicidal thinking. In some instances, suicide becomes the "last word" in an argument. It can be a way to punish a spouse, parent, friend, or even a child for some wound or insult. If anger can be an expression of self-centeredness, then suicide is an aggressive act of self-absorption.[2]

A person's theological self-centeredness can be seen in the fact that suicide is an extreme expression of self-declared autonomy. It stands in contrast to the way the Bible portrays human beings, as those who know they exist as creatures in relationship with a Creator. As creatures we are designed, maintained, and owned by God. Creation expresses his design (Ps. 139:13) and God actively maintains our existence (Col. 1:17). Creation brings God pleasure by expressing his glory (Ps. 148:7). In short, God owns everything. The charge given to humanity over creation and over our own bodies is a stewardship (Gen. 1:28). How much of this, however, do we actively know and respond to?

Romans 1 suggests that a person—believer or unbeliever—who contemplates suicide must actively suppress the Spirit's testimony that he is a creature made in the image of God, living in dependence on him. General revelation (Rom. 1:18–20) reveals more than God's existence and attributes, however. It also bears witness to his righteous moral decrees (Rom. 1:32: "Although they know God's righteous decrees that those who do such things deserve death . . ."). The command against murder given to Noah after the flood (Gen. 9:6) isn't new information; it confirms what the sinful heart knows but suppresses. Man images God. And God alone defines the boundaries of human life (Job 14:5).

Of course, depressed Christians I counsel would probably agree that they are creatures who are dependent on God for life. They would probably even agree that they are made in the image and likeness of God, although they might have difficulty believing that other biblical truths apply to them. But would they have a palpable awareness of their status as image-bearers? Would that awareness control their behavior? Paul's statement that human beings know that the violation of God's righteous decrees brings judgment implies that we must suppress an awareness of condemnation and death. It is not unlike, perhaps, the sense of fear and dread that cuts through us when death touches our families or hovers over our own lives in a serious illness. The suicidal person must quench the Spirit's testimony in that regard. For surely God speaks loud and often to the suicidal believer, not only about being a creature, but about the covenant made on his behalf: that he has been purchased by blood, and that beyond being a creature, the blood purchase makes him part of the family of God. God has a unique proprietary interest in him (1 Cor. 6:19–20). For that reason, we want to demolish the idea that someone who takes his life is a sad, wounded, and weakened victim, and that suicide is a noble expression of his fragility and God's failure to rescue him.

Common Features in Suicidal Thinking

What perspectives reinforce a suicidal person's distorted view of life? Some common features of suicidal thinking include:

- Extreme psychological pain related to unmet psychological needs.
- A view of self that says she cannot tolerate such intense pain.
- An overwhelming feeling of hopelessness, and the belief that she is helpless to solve problems.
- A sense of isolation or desertion accompanied by the belief that others cannot, should not, or do not want to offer support, nurture, or care.
- A repetitive thought that ending life is the only way to escape the pain or the problem.

When considering these features, bear in mind that they are not unique to suicide. Most are typical features of depression, though perhaps experienced in a more intense or prolonged way when someone is suicidal. More importantly, no single feature is likely to cause someone to kill herself. I know many people with chronic and pervasive psychological pain. Not all of them are suicidal. I know many people who feel hopeless and helpless. Not all of them are suicidal. Suicide appears to be linked to the *interplay* of these elements. That is, a sense of hopelessness, combined with a pattern of poor coping, a limited tolerance for pain, and a flight from help all join in some way to lead someone to plan a suicide. Moreover, these categories are interdependent in various ways. For example, hopelessness can be both a *source* of psychological pain and a *result*. A person's belief in her inability to change things is probably bound up with her experience that the pain is intolerable. Remember, in an ultimate sense, these elements do not cause anything at all. They point to the state of the believer's heart and her relationship with Christ.

Suicide should be understood as a multi-determined event. A more formal definition can help us connect assessment with intervention: *Suicide is the product of a continuous transaction between the person's heart, his symptoms of depression, the levels and types of stressors in his environment, and the strategies he uses to cope with his depression and life circumstances.*

Intense psychological pain. The common impetus behind suicide is the person's sense of unendurable psychological pain. The goal of suicide is often simply to end that pain: "I just want the pain to go away." Death is a means to an end, not an end in itself. "I just want to die" most often means, "I want to stop feeling bad."

Psychological pain is difficult to define and impossible to quantify. Nevertheless, the level of pain the person experiences is a crucial factor in suicidal intent. Most of us have known emotional pain or distress at one time or another. Scripture presents it in various ways, such as the poignant descriptions in the Psalms (e.g., 22, 38, 42). When asked to describe their psychological pain, counselees may say things like, "It's a heavy feeling . . . I feel like I am carrying a weight on my chest," but they normally distinguish between psychological pain and physical complaints. In fact, they often report that psychological pain leads to secondary physical pain, like headaches and nausea.

As they try to identify the source of the pain, depressed persons may connect it to specific experiences (guilt, shame, loneliness, alienation, abandonment, hopelessness), but will frequently regard it as a pain that overshadows everything. They will also describe their pain in terms of its debilitating effects, both internal (loss of concentration, new fears, inability to make decisions) and external (unemployment, loss of friendships, financial ruin). The extent to which a person sees pain as something ruining his life, especially when he believes that life will be this way forever, is part of the network of beliefs that leads to suicide.

You can help the person think about this pain more constructively by helping him compare his view of the pain with God's view. Depressed people who report feeling suicidal normally associate their pain with some thwarted felt need. Second, they have come to believe that they cannot endure the pain associated with that "unmet need." Third, they feel hopeless, that they cannot change themselves or the situation.

Abuse of medication. Because pain and consciousness are linked together, it is important to find out how much the person has already tried to manage pain by controlling consciousness. Often a person will use hypnotic/sedative medication to alter his level of consciousness and manage pain. Ask about the use of anti-anxiety agents (e.g., Valium, Ativan, Klonipin), over-the-counter medications with calming or sedating properties, alcohol, or anything the person thinks will render him less aware or make the feelings less intense.

Overdoses of medication that result in life-threatening medical crises may reflect the person's desire to take an emotional vacation. In these instances, she will often guess at a dosage that will put her to sleep "for a while" without a conscious intention to die. Not all overdoses are botched suicide attempts or cries for help. They do pose a concern, however, for several reasons. First, mistakes in self-medication can be lethal. The person may presume that "more" is better at removing her as far from the pain as possible. Even people with medical backgrounds can succumb to this distorted thinking. Second, escapism is a common feature of depression and is habit-forming. While there are no annual, national data comparing suicide attempts with completed suicides, the research estimates that there are 8–25 attempted suicides to one completion. The ratio is higher in women and youth and lower in men and the elderly. It is safe to say that habitual self-medication is a "dry run" that will make it easier for the person to commit suicide if her intentions change.

A *situational crisis*. A situational crisis normally acts as a catalyst to suicide, becoming a focal point for the person's thoughts and emotions. Situational crises could include:

- Financial problems due to unemployment, mismanagement, debt, or substance abuse.
- Serious illness of a family member that places great demands on the rest of the family.
- Death of a family member or friend, and unresolved grief.
- Marital conflict, physical abuse, separation or divorce.
- Public disgrace or exposure, perhaps the result of immoral or illegal activity.

In some cases, particularly if there is a history of chronic depression, a person may have helped to create the problem. Unemployment due to habitual drunkenness can be a catalyst for suicide for the person or the spouse. In other instances, problems beyond the person's control will reinforce a sense of helplessness.

Distorted thinking. The nature or extent of the problem is often subject to distorted thinking. Problems may seem catastrophic when they are not. Predictions about the future can become arbitrary and unrealistic. Possibilities are unrealistically narrowed (tunnel vision), and reasoning about persons and events become rigidly all-or-nothing. Suicidal thinking typically insists that there are only two choices: pain or cessation of consciousness.[3]

Where does all this anguish come from?[4] It is created and sustained by thwarted desires that a person experiences as felt needs: "I *need* what I have lost and have no hope of getting." These hopeless cravings may relate to a particular life circumstance or a person's life overall. For example, a man may experience a devastating loss of security (or status, identity, control, or freedom) because of catastrophic financial troubles: "I *need* the security that money provided, and without it life has become unbearable." A woman facing marital betrayal or a broken relationship with a parent may despair over the loss of love, affirmation, and nurture: "I *need* to be loved by that person; without him I'm in free fall." A teenager experiences a profound sense of shame and worthlessness over a failure to achieve in school (or sports, or romance): "I *need* to get As, and these Bs are proof of terminal inferiority. I may as well end it all now." The situation alone—poverty, rejection, failure—does not constitute the crisis. It is the life-dominating desire that interprets the situation that turns loss into hopelessness and then suicide.

How Can You Help?

Consider a man who wants to kill himself because his wife has left him. He is crushed by a sense of loss, shame, self-pity, guilt, and anguish. He is also consumed by an impotent anger at what his wife has done. Suicide seems like the only way out—and the only way to get even. How will you help him?

First, acknowledge the reality of his pain. In a crisis, the need for empathy increases, not lessens. Recognizing the intensity of his anguish does not mean that you are validating his desire to kill himself or his distorted thinking.

You will not ease his misery or banish thoughts of suicide by telling him that things are not so bad! Simply acknowledging his experience and emotions often helps to ease them.

Second, help him see the connection between his pain and his felt need (not between his pain and his circumstance), without immediately challenging what he lives for. I often help a person rephrase need language into a vocabulary of feared consequences. For example, "I can't live without my wife" becomes "Life without my wife will be unbearable because _____." In that instance, a suicidal man had said that death would be preferable to the shame of telling his family about his impending divorce. A person's response may also center on perceived lack of ability. A woman intended to take her life because her husband had recently died and he had always taken care of everything. We reframed her intent as, "I don't want to live because I don't think I will ever be able to manage the finances." In a third instance, suicidal intent was reframed as, "I don't want to live because divorce means I am unlovable." The specific naming of the felt need often reveals it for what it is, and starts to break its hold.

Third, challenge constricted options and irrational thoughts. Help people identify ways in which their thinking is full of contradictions and falsehoods. I might ask the Christian divorcé, "How have you dealt with your own failure and guilt before? Have you ever found God merciful to you? Are your failures so big that they are unpardonable? Have you ever forgiven another for his offenses—even if the wrongs were minor compared to what your wife has done? If Jesus Christ can forgive you, can he help you forgive your wife rather than destroy yourself in hopelessness and bitterness? Is suicide really your only option? Is getting even really your only option? Are your only two choices either unbearable pain or self-inflicted death?" I will ask what beliefs and ideas control his thoughts. What is he thinking, and are those things true?

I will also ask about attempted solutions, strategies already tried that "didn't work." What made them unworkable? What is his definition of "worked" and "didn't work"? Does he have a false and impossible definition of success? Or does he have the right definition, but an expectation of instant results? Some people simply give up too early, or attempt something beyond their abilities (such as "to change another person"), or try something without encouragement, instruction, and support. Offering to help someone carry out a workable strategy will often help him out of a suicidal crisis. Offering true options and beliefs can help such a person see his situation in a very different light.

Fourth, explore his perceptions of hopelessness. Intellectually, hopelessness is the utter certainty that there is no solution to a problem, and the loss of what he values is certain. He *sees* no hope. Emotionally, hopelessness is a pervasive despair and misery, or dread of the future. He *feels* no hope. Research shows that hopelessness is the single strongest predictor of suicide. It plays the deciding role in predicting which heavy drinkers would attempt suicide.[5] It is a better predictor of suicide intent among drug abusers than depression.[6] Among the very depressed, hopelessness is the difference between feeling very down and suicidal intent.[7]

From God's point of view, there *are* people who have good reason to have no hope: "What the wicked fears will come upon him, . . . the expectation of the wicked perishes" (Prov. 10:24, 28 NASB). But Jesus Christ creates a revolution. For those who have God as their Father and Christ as their Redeemer, "The desire of the righteous will be granted. . . . The hope of the righteous is gladness" (Prov. 10:24, 28 NASB). If a person has Christ, he has hope that will not go away, that will pursue him and never let him go, that will make a decisive difference in the long run. Believers in Christ are the most hope-filled people on the planet, for solid reasons. If a Christian is without hope and sees himself as helpless, it underscores that his thinking is out of alignment with God's.

Hopelessness is a failure to recognize the wisdom of God. Faith involves a belief in God's goodness and wisdom. Our level of faith is revealed when the path before us is difficult. On several occasions I have counseled men who have admitted to sexual sin with a child. The choices before them have brought some to the brink of suicide. The prospects of exposure, humiliation, financial hardship, criminal prosecution, and the loss of family come with owning the sin. Hopelessness enters in when we refuse to trust that God desires the best for his children. Our ministry goal is that they will rely on God's mercy in Christ, and that God will honor their repentance. The Bible portrays humiliated men who still had hope: Psalm 32, Luke 23:39–43.

Hopelessness is also a failure to desire what God desires. James 4 portrays conflict as a war of desires (vv. 1–3). Frustration enters in when we sinfully put our hope in fleshly desires and God thwarts our pursuit of those desires. He calls us instead to desire better things and to live out a fundamental gratitude in Christ (Phil. 3:7–15; 4:3–9; Col. 2:6ff; 3:1–4).

Hopelessness is an unwillingness to view time as God does. It enters in when we look for our hope and reward in this present age, even though God calls us to live with a view towards eternity. I will explore this with the suicidal man: Does he set his hope on his wife or Christ? His reputation or Christ? Her changing or Christ? This is an issue that the Bible relentlessly pursues: Romans 8:18–24; 2 Corinthians 4:17–18; 5:7–8; Hebrews 11:1; 1 Peter 1:13ff.

Fifth, help the person to separate pain and need by reframing his understanding of the nature and source of his "felt needs." When we adopt the view that needs are what motivate us, and that pain and psychological difficulties are due to unmet or thwarted needs, we ignore the role that sin plays in our experience of life. The man abandoned by his wife does not *need* her. It hurts to lose her, yes. It's hard. It's humiliating. There are fears and heartaches that only the Last Day will soothe. But he has no *need* to kill himself. Psalm 73 is as true today as it has always been.

Just as important as the crisis itself is the value or significance the person places on the event. Rejection, for example, means different things to different people. If I allow other people to define who I am, then their rejection will be devastating. But if I don't depend on their approval for my own self-concept, then failure or rejection is less traumatic (1 Cor. 4:1–4). More importantly, if I recognize that the way I deal with people's perceptions is a byproduct of my sin nature, I actually can grow from the experience of rejection.

How to Assess the Risk of Suicide

There are so many contexts in which one might have to evaluate someone's wish to die that any set of guidelines or procedures I might offer is somewhat arbitrary. Making an evaluation on a telephone hot line is far more difficult than evaluating a church member you know well. Still, certain basic predictors apply in most cases, and I have tried to include them here.

Presenting Problem. Assessment should normally begin by reviewing the event that triggered the crisis. This is what the person is most concerned about. Sometimes you may be tempted to skip this discussion because you suspect that she is at risk and you want to ask about her depression or suicidal intent. But usually this will frustrate her, because, for her, the event *is* the reason. Unless the person has already acted out a suicidal impulse or an action seems imminent, it is usually better to get a fuller picture that includes the events weighing heavily on her mind.

Background Information. Try to place the particular crisis within the context of the person's life history: relationship with Christ, pattern of successful and unsuccessful coping skills, impact that character and personality patterns are likely to have on the problem, other kinds of problems, previous counseling experiences, brief medical history, disrupted sleep patterns, and so on.

Substance Abuse as a Risk Factor. There is a strong connection between substance abuse and suicide. Data reported by the National Institutes of Mental Health indicate that the strongest risk factors for attempted suicides in adults are depression, alcohol abuse, cocaine use, and separation and divorce. The strongest risk factors for attempted suicide in youth are depression, alcohol or drug abuse, and aggressive or disruptive behaviors.[8] Someone who attempts suicide is likely to have a preexisting drug or alcohol problem. This does not mean that anyone with a drinking or drug problem is likely to kill herself or that substance abuse causes suicide. But be aware that the two often go hand-in-hand.

The incidence of substance abuse among evangelical Christians is likely to be less than the general population, and possibly less in the subgroup of depressed or suicidal Christians. To evaluate substance abuse as a risk factor or predictor of suicide with Christians, consider the following:

- Present level of use
- Length of abstinence
- Level of temptation to use reported by the person
- Involvement with drug/alcohol support groups

Individuals who report drug or alcohol use as recent as six months can be regarded as high risk if their substance abuse is associated with their depression. The role that substances play in the way the person deals with stressful circumstances or distressing feelings should be evaluated individually. The level of impairment is also significant: people who use drugs or alcohol to get "wasted" when they feel bad are already altering their levels of consciousness to get relief. Frequent use can also aggravate depression, leading to a vicious, sinful cycle of irresponsibility, blame-shifting, depressed mood, further withdrawal, and so on.

Available Resources. Ask the person about her support system, including family, friends, church ministry, and previous counselors. People who know the individual well can tell you about previous bouts of depression, suicide attempts, etc. Friends or family members should be interviewed out of the person's hearing. They can sometimes be more objective about her experiences, and may be able to supply a chronology of her problems. This will help you gauge how much help they could offer in a crisis.

Suicidal Thinking and Intention. Evaluating suicidal intent is not easy. Things are not always what they seem. It is true that thought precedes action, but it is not necessarily true that more suicidal thinking means a higher likelihood of suicidal behavior. Generalities are only guidelines; they cannot replace wisdom and discernment. D. C. Clark and J. Fawcett propose developing an "ascending" inquiry about suicidal thoughts and behaviors.[9] This means that you should begin by asking very general questions about suicidal thinking that the person will be likely to admit to, and then explore the extent to which her thoughts have progressed to details and plans.

Since pain is the impetus behind most suicidal acts, I propose evaluating the person's felt experience first. Assigning some value to her pain can help evaluate the likelihood of suicide.

I usually ask people to assign a number to their pain (1–10), and give me descriptive adjectives for each number. I often ask them to specifically assign a number to "unbearability." I usually ask a depressed and suicidal person to associate pain level and problem-solving strategies. What do you do when you are feeling level 4 pain? What would make level 4 pain go away? How could you reduce level 6 pain, associated with the fact that you just lost your lob, to level 2? This helps not only to identify the person's subjectively defined level of pain, it also reveals whether she believes that the pain cannot be escaped. The basic rule of suicide intervention is this: if the level of suffering can be reduced a little, the individual might choose to live.

In evaluating suicidal intent, you might say to the person, "When people feel this way, it isn't unusual for them to wish they were dead so the pain would go away. Have you ever had thoughts like that?" Most depressed people think about suicide from time to time and would therefore answer affirmatively.

The next step is to determine how often the person has suicidal thoughts and how intense or compelling they are. This involves asking the person if she has ever talked with someone else about suicide. People preoccupied with killing themselves will often tell someone about it directly or indirectly. Intent can also be explored by asking how the person feels about upcoming events and by taking note of any change of behavior, such as giving valued possessions away or having a sudden interest in clearing up old debts or conflicts.

Planning a suicide involves choosing a method, obtaining what's needed to carry it out, and arranging ways to prevent interruption or intervention. You might ask the person to name the different ways she has thought of killing herself—shooting, drowning, overdose, hanging, etc. Then, working from that list, discuss each method in the order in which they were presented. The idea is to explore how much time the person has spent working out the details of a suicide by that method. When an individual seems engrossed with one particular method, and especially when she has begun to schedule or rehearse suicide according to that plan, she is at high risk. Has she gotten what she needs to carry out the plan? Does her plan minimize the probability of interruption? How much medical damage is likely if her attempt fails?

You should also ask if the person has ever experimented with suicidal behaviors. Has she ever taken a few pills to see what it feels like, tied things around her neck, driven at high speed, or practiced with an unloaded gun? Dry runs help the person to resolve any ambivalence she might feel about suicide. These experimental actions are some of the strongest indicators that a suicide is about to happen. When questioned about the dry run, the person may talk about why she doesn't want to kill herself and deny that the actions mean anything. Dry runs, however, are strong indicators of intent and should not be dismissed.

A Noble End. Sometimes a person reflects on the value of life, reasons for living, and reasons to die, and develops a false notion of the nobility of her death. Dying may seem like an unselfish act that allows her loved ones to be less burdened and thus able to get on with their lives. An anorectic woman once told me that suicide was an "authentic act of control" over her life. She wanted to assign some aesthetic beauty to her initiative. This should be regarded as an ominous indicator and the person as an extremely high risk.

In the years I have been involved in biblical counseling, I have not completely fathomed the hopelessness and despair in a believer that makes death more attractive than life. I pray that my inability is not merely a lack of empathy for someone who struggles. I hope that it is a vision for Christ and his kingdom that keeps the true "meaning" of suicide out of my reach. As biblical counselors, we hold Paul's view about the sorrows and struggles of life before the church, and pray with hope that we never need to help someone else make sense of the senseless.

Notes

1 G. C. Berkouwer, *Studies in Dogmatics: Sin* (Grand Rapids: Eerdmans, 1971), pp. 134–35.

2 Suicide's inner logic also varies across cultures, as well as between individuals. Get your facts.

3 Studies of suicidal people often describe such distortions, e.g., A. Beck, A. Weissman, and M. Kovacs, "Alcoholism, Hopelessness and Suicidal Behavior," *Journal of Studies on Alcohol*, 37(1), 1976; E. S. Shneidman, *Definition of Suicide* (New York: John Wiley and Sons, 1985).

4 Edward T. Welch, "Exalting Pain? Ignoring Pain? What Do We Do with Suffering?" *Journal of Biblical Counseling*, 12:3, 1999.

5 Beck, et al.

6 G. D. Emery, R. A. Steer, and A. Beck, "Depression, Hopelessness and Suicidal Intent among Heroin Addicts," *International Journal of Addictions*, 16(3), 1981, pp. 425–29.

7 M. Kovacs, A. Beck, and A. Weissman, "Hopelessness: An Indicator of Suicidal Risk," *Suicide and Life-threatening Behavior* 5(2), 1975, pp. 98–103.

8 D. C. Clark and J. Fawcett, "Suicide Risk Assessment and Prediction in the 1990s," *Crisis*, 11, 1992, pp. 104–12.

9 Ibid.

Jeffrey S. Black *is a pastor at Calvary Chapel in Philadelphia and adjunct faculty member of the Christian Counseling and Educational Foundation's School of Biblical Counseling in Glenside, Pennsylvania.*

RCL Ministry Booklets

Pornography: Slaying the Dragon, by David Powlison

Pre-Engagement: 5 Questions to Ask Yourselves, by David Powlison and John Yenchko

Priorities: Mastering Time Management, by James C. Petty

Procrastination: First Steps to Change, by Walter Henegar

Self-Injury: When Pain Feels Good, by Edward T. Welch

Sexual Sin: Combatting the Drifting and Cheating, by Jeffrey S. Black

Stress: Peace amid Pressure, by David Powlison

Suffering: Eternity Makes a Difference, by Paul David Tripp

Suicide: Understanding and Intervening, by Jeffrey S. Black

Teens and Sex: How Should We Teach Them? by Paul David Tripp

Thankfulness: Even When It Hurts, by Susan Lutz

Why Me?: Comfort for the Victimized, by David Powlison

Worry: Pursuing a Better Path to Peace, by David Powlison